Books should be returned on or before the
last date stamped below

-6 MAR 2004

-8 JUL

12 OCT 2004

D1080150

1222358

WHAT'S SO GOOD

about vegetables?

By Ronne Randall

helping to explain nutrition

WHAT'S SO GOOD

about vegetables?

J613.2

1222358

ticktock
MEDIA

Copyright © ticktock Entertainment Ltd 2003

First published in Great Britain in 2003 by ticktock Media Ltd.,

Unit 2, Orchard Business Centre, North Farm Road, Tunbridge Wells, Kent, TN2 3XF

We would like to thank: Lorna Cowan, Sarah Schenker at the British Nutrition

Foundation and Elizabeth Wiggans.

ISBN 1 86007 385 9 pbk

ISBN 1 86007 391 3 hbk

Printed in Egypt

A CIP catalogue record for this book is available from the British Library.

CONTENTS

Any words appearing in the text in bold,
like this, are explained in the Glossary.

Food tastes good and
it can be fun to eat.
But why is food
good for our bodies?

Food makes us feel better when we are hungry.
But can it make you grow bigger?
Or help you play your favourite sport for longer?

Eating a **balanced diet** with lots of different foods
will give your body all the **nutrients** that it needs.

The meal below has a good mix of the nutrients
you need to keep you healthy and
make you strong.

Salad

Milk

Fruit with ice cream

Meatballs with tomato sauce

Bread and butter

Spaghetti (pasta)

What's so good about bread?

Bread is a **carbohydrate** food.

Bread and butter

So is pasta, rice and cereal. Crackers and potatoes are carbohydrate foods too.

These foods give you long-lasting **energy**. They help you run and play without getting tired right away.

6

They also give you **fibre** which helps your **digestive system** work smoothly.

Some carbohydrate treats are popcorn, your favourite sandwich or a baked potato.

This is the "Balance of Good Health Plate". It shows you how much of each type of food to eat each day.

This much food should be carbohydrate foods every day.

What country does spaghetti come from? (answer on page 23)

7

What's so good about vegetables?

Vegetables like crisp lettuce, cool cucumber, crunchy carrots and leafy spinach are real super-foods.

Salad

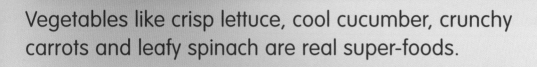

They all have important **vitamins** and **minerals** that your body needs.

Vitamin A, from carrots and spinach, helps your eyes to see better in the dark.

B Vitamins help your body turn food into **energy**.

Which "vegetable" is actually a fruit? (answer on page 23)

The mineral potassium, found in peas and cucumbers, helps your muscles work.

Like **carbohydrate** foods, vegetables have **fibre** to keep your **digestive system** happy!

There are lots of great ways to enjoy vegetables. Try pizza with vegetable toppings, or crunchy carrot and celery sticks with dip. Tomato or vegetable soup is good too!

Carbohydrate foods

You should try to eat at least 5 **portions** of vegetables and fruit every day.

What's so good about fruit?

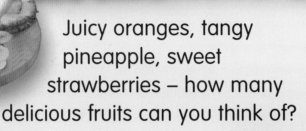

Fruit

Juicy oranges, tangy pineapple, sweet strawberries – how many delicious fruits can you think of?

All fruits are packed with **vitamins** that help to keep you well.

Fruits like oranges have lots of Vitamin C.

It is important because it keeps your gums healthy.

Vitamin C helps your body's defences keep you well – fighting **infections** and diseases.

Some fun ways to fill up on fruit are fruit kebabs, fruit smoothies and fruit pie.

Carbohydrate foods

Which "fruit" is really a vegetable?

(answer on page 23)

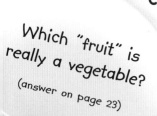

You should try to eat at least 5 **portions** of fruit and vegetables every day.

What's so good about meat?

Meat – like meatballs, turkey, chicken, lamb chops and steak – has lots of **protein**.

Meatballs

So do fish, eggs, baked beans and nuts.

Your body uses protein to make new muscle and skin **cells**.

Some people don't eat meat or fish. Do you know what they are called?

(answer on page 23)

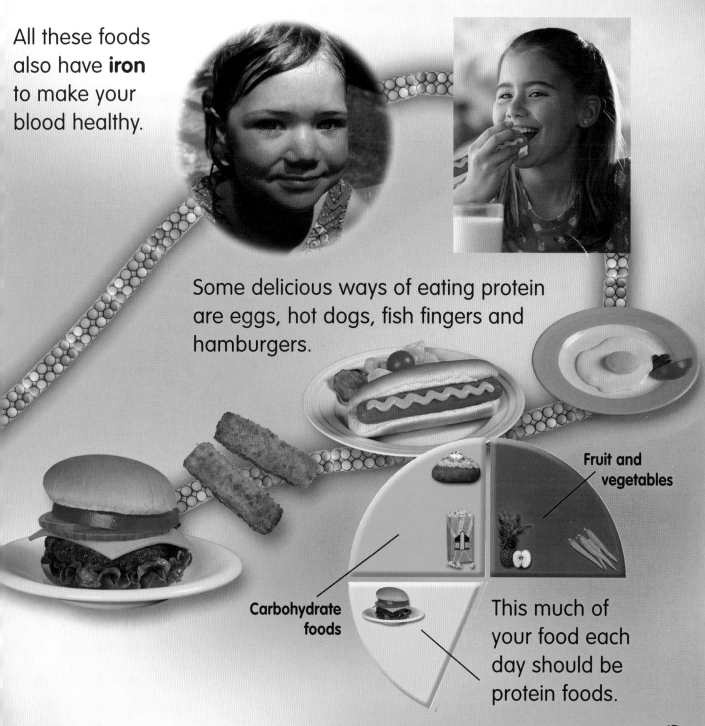

All these foods also have **iron** to make your blood healthy.

Some delicious ways of eating protein are eggs, hot dogs, fish fingers and hamburgers.

Fruit and vegetables

Carbohydrate foods

This much of your food each day should be protein foods.

What's so good about milk?

Dairy products like yogurt, ice cream and cheese are all made from milk.

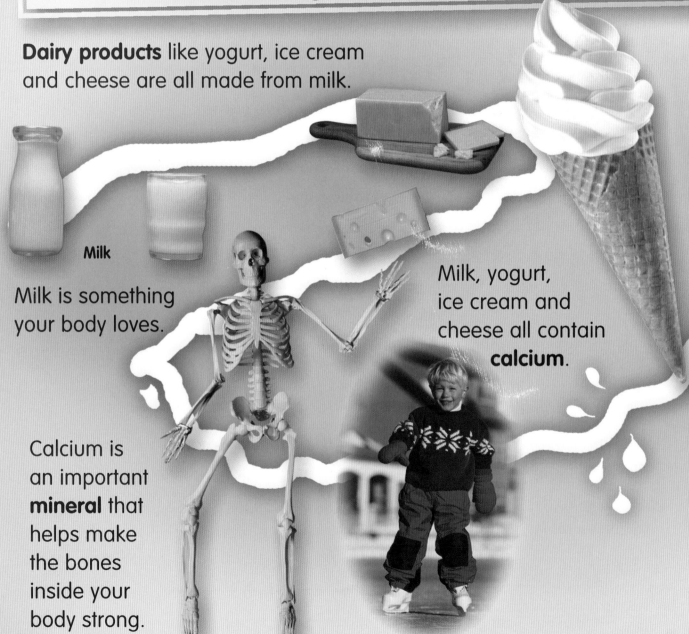

Milk

Milk is something your body loves.

Milk, yogurt, ice cream and cheese all contain **calcium**.

Calcium is an important **mineral** that helps make the bones inside your body strong.

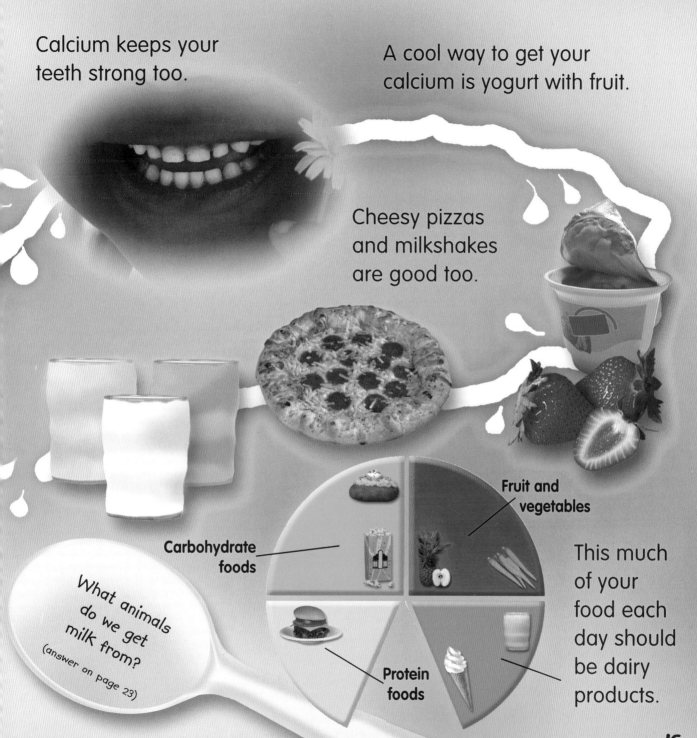

Calcium keeps your teeth strong too.

A cool way to get your calcium is yogurt with fruit.

Cheesy pizzas and milkshakes are good too.

What animals do we get milk from?

(answer on page 23)

Carbohydrate foods

Fruit and vegetables

Protein foods

This much of your food each day should be dairy products.

What's so good about butter?

Butter and margarine have lots of **fat**.

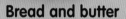

Bread and butter

We all need some of the fat in butter, margarine and vegetable oils.

Fat helps you to **absorb** some of the **vitamins** from the other foods you eat.

But too much fat is bad for you.

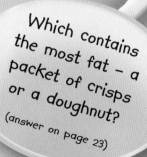

Which contains the most fat – a packet of crisps or a doughnut?

(answer on page 23)

There are other foods that have lots of fat. They also have lots of sugar and salt.

Once in a while, it's OK to have sweets, biscuits and crisps – as a treat!

But remember to leave room for all the good things your body needs.

Carbohydrate foods

Fruit and vegetables

Protein foods

Dairy products

Foods containing fat and sugar

And remember to brush your teeth at least twice a day to keep them healthy!

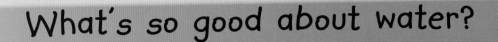

What's so good about water?

Your body is made up of lots of things – skin, hair, bones, muscles, blood and water.

If you weigh 18 kilos, 12 kilos of that is water!

But your body keeps losing some of that water.

Exercise that makes you sweat, going to the toilet, even just breathing – all these make you lose water.

Your body tells you that you've lost a lot of water by making you thirsty.

Even before you feel thirsty, you should drink water and other **fluids** like fruit juice, squash or milk, to put back what you've lost.

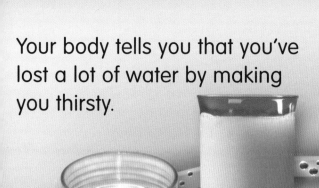

You can get some water by eating fruits and vegetables with lots of water in them. Good ones to choose are tomatoes, grapes, cucumber and melon.

You should drink 6-8 glasses of fluids every day.

Which fruit or vegetable contains the most water?

(answer on page 23)

Where does my food go?

Now you know that food isn't just good to eat and fun – it's good for your body too!

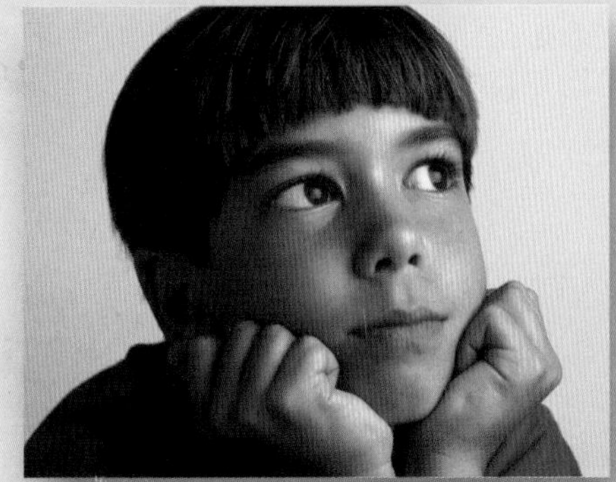

Vitamins, minerals and fibre

Fat

Carbohydrates and fibre

Calcium

Protein

But how does all that goodness get to where it needs to go?

The answer is **digestion** – the way your food gets broken down so your body can use it.

1. First, the food goes into your mouth where it mixes with **saliva** when you chew.

4. Your small intestine **absorbs nutrients** from the food, and sends them into your body to do their work.

2. Next, the food goes down a tube called the oesophagus into your stomach.

5. Your large intestine absorbs water from the food and turns anything left into waste.

3. The food is all mashed up into a kind of soup in your stomach.

6. The waste leaves your body when you go to the toilet.

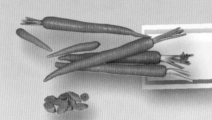

Glossary

Absorb To take something in so it can be used.

Balanced diet Meals and snacks that include foods from all the food groups in the right amounts. They will give you all the nutrients you need to stay healthy.

Calcium A mineral that helps make bones and teeth strong.

Carbohydrate An important nutrient that the body uses for energy. Carbohydrates come from foods like bread, pasta and cereal, and from fruits and vegetables.

Cells The smallest building blocks of living things. Your body is made of cells.

Dairy products Milk and foods made from milk, such as cheese and yogurt.

Digestion The way your body breaks down food so it can be used.

Digestive system All the parts of your body that take part in digestion.

Energy The ability to be active and do things. Your body uses energy even when you are asleep.

Fat A nutrient that provides energy, and helps your body absorb some vitamins.

Fibre A kind of carbohydrate that your body can't digest. It helps move foods through your digestive system.

Fluids Anything you can drink.

Infections Illnesses or sores caused by germs.

Iron A mineral found in meat, spinach, dried beans, apricots and some other foods. It helps

make your blood healthy.

Minerals Special substances that come from water, soil and rocks, and cannot be made by living things. We get minerals from plants which take them in from water and soil, and from animals that eat plants.

Nutrients The goodness in food which your body needs to grow and to work properly.

Portions The amount of any food that you eat at one time. You can see how much a portion is on this page.

Protein A nutrient that helps your body make new cells and repair old ones. It is needed for growth.

Saliva The liquid made in your mouth which starts the digestion of your food.

Vitamins Special substances found in tiny amounts in our food. They help our bodies turn the food we eat into energy to keep the body healthy.

Here are the portion sizes for the main food groups. One portion =

carbohydrates: 1 slice of bread; tbsp cooked rice or pasta; small bowl dry cereal.

fruits and vegetables: tbsp chopped fruits or vegetables; 1 tbsp leafy vegetables; 1 piece of fruit; small glass fruit juice; tbsp dried fruit.

protein: 1 medium burger; 2 fishfingers; 1 egg; tbsp baked beans; 2 tablespoons peanut butter.

dairy products: 1 pot milk or yogurt; piece of cheese the size of a pack of cards.

(tbsp = tablespoon)

Could you answer all the questions? Here are the answers:

Page 7: Spaghetti comes from Italy.

Page 8: Tomatoes are actually fruits.

Page 11: Rhubarb is really a vegetable.

Page 12: People who don't eat meat and fish are called vegetarians.

Page 15: We get milk from cows, and sometimes from goats and sheep.

Page 16: A doughnut contains more fat than a packet of crisps.

Page 19: Cucumber contains the most water.

Index

t=top, b=bottom, c=centre, l=left, r=right,
OFC=outside front cover, OBC=outside back cover

Alamy images: 4bl, 11tr, 13tr, 16bl. Comstock: 14bl, 24bl.
Corbis: 1tl, 1tc, 1tr, 1cr, 1br, 1bl, 1cl, 1c, 2tl, 2tr, 2br, 2bl, 3tl, 3tr, 3br, 3bl, 4tl, 4tc, 4tr, 4br, 4cl, 5tr, 5b, 6t, 6br, 6bl, 7tr, 7c, 8tl, 8tr, 8bl, 9t, 9tr, 9b, 10tl, 10tr, 10cl, 10b, 11c, 12tl, 12tr, 12c, 12b, 13tc, 13cr, 13cl, 13b, 14tl, 14tr, 14br, 15tl, 15c, 16tl, 16r, 17tl, 17tc, 17tr, 18tl, 18br, 18bl, 19tl, 19cr, 19bl, 20t, 20bl, 22tl, 22tr, 22br, 22cr, 22bl, 23tl, 23tc, 23bc, 23bl, 24tr. Creatas: OFC.

Every effort has been made to trace the copyright holders and we apologize in advance for any unintentional omissions. We would be pleased to insert the appropriate acknowledgements in any subsequent edition of this publication.